TIM PAGE'S NAM

Introduction by William Shawcross

For Dr. Jacob Mathis,
for my father who never saw it,
and for all those who never made it back

THIS IS A BORZOI BOOK
PUBLISHED BY ALFRED A. KNOPF, INC.

Text and photographs Copyright © 1983 by Tim Page
Introduction Copyright © 1983 by William Shawcross

All rights reserved under International and Pan-
American Copyright Conventions. Published in the
United States by Alfred A. Knopf, Inc., New York, and
simultaneously in Canada by Random House of
Canada Limited, Toronto. Distributed by Random
House, Inc., New York.

Library of Congress Cataloging in Publication Data

Page, Tim.
Nam.

   1. Vietnamese Conflict, 1961–1975——United States.
I. Title.
DS558.P33 1983   959.704'33'73   82–48704
ISBN 0–394–53005–5
ISBN 0–394–71345–1 pbk

Manufactured in Japan
First Edition

Six years after the war had ended, I returned to Saigon. Although I never lived there for any length of time, it was like going back to somewhere intensely familiar and also passionately exhilarating.

There was a brand-new airport-terminal building to replace the congested rabbit-hutch affair through which one had had to hustle past the immigration officers of the Thieu government. At the entrance to the airport, the cement block which had read, fantastically, "The noble sacrifice of allied soldiers will never be forgotten," was still standing. The promise, long since wept away, had been whitewashed out, but one could still detect the letters beneath the peeling paint.

The road into town was much quieter now – there were no armored or American cars, and there were far more bicycles than the Hondas which had previously clogged the streets. The air was much cleaner.

But the streets were hauntingly familiar. The main road, Tu Do, which ran from the Continental Hotel – where one could sit on the terrace to drink and dream or talk or write – down to the port on the Saigon river, still had a certain bustle. There were still stalls selling lacquer or ivory or cigarettes or peanuts. Trade was not so brisk as before, but there were still large, ungainly, ill-dressed foreigners sauntering around. They were not Americans; they were Soviets or East Europeans. It soon became clear that the Russians were not very popular. "Americans without dollars," the Vietnamese called them. The one Vietnamese phrase I now needed was *Kung Fai Lien Xo* – "I am not a Russian." That brought instant smiles, though many people were disappointed to learn that I was only from Britain, not from America.

The false fronts of the old bars in which wretched GIs had fumbled wretched bar girls had been removed, but many of the bars were still operating, and there were still young men and women drinking in them. The difference was that the men were Vietnamese and few if any of the girls were prostitutes.

But most extraordinary of all was the music. In the bars were the huge and rather ugly wooden-case stereo systems which had been fashionable fifteen years ago, and from them came the music of the 'sixties and early 'seventies, blaring with irony across a decade and more. The Grateful Dead, The Doors,

Jimi Hendrix, The Beach Boys, The Stones – there they were, all stacked up and being played with a strange nostalgia by Vietnamese who hated Russians and who could only have been children when the songs were recorded and brought to their country by a vast and absurd, frightened and cruel army of occupation. That music was an essential part of the Vietnam – or 'Nam as he and many GIs called it – in which Tim Page lived; one of the sections of this book is called Rock and Roll Flash.

Page must have been crazy before he had half his brain blown away. The mad journalist who is waiting at the top of the river in the film *Apocalypse Now* was the creation of Page's friend Michael Herr and is based partly on Page. His childhood was spent in Orpington, a dull London suburb, and he says it was very happy. Nonetheless, one day when he was seventeen his parents found his room empty and a note saying he had gone to see the world, maybe join the Merchant Marine, and would they please cancel his driving test. They kept the note.

He took the mid-'sixties land-route east, but instead of remaining in Katmandu he journeyed on to Laos where a small secret war was being fought – 1965. He picked up a camera, snapped some exclusive shots of one of the many Lao coups, sold them to UPI and began to learn the business. He seemed good and UPI sent him on to Vietnam where the American buildup was still only building and when names like Danang, Khe Sanh and Tet were still unknown to the world.

Page and his friends spent a lot of the time "goofing around," in his phrase. Like most journalists in Vietnam they thought and said they were opposed to the American effort. But at the same time, they set out to have themselves a ball of a war. To more conventional journalists they seemed like war groupies, high on the dope, the death, the destruction, the gear, the astonishing privileges that Vietnam and the U.S. Army offered to correspondents. Page would not deny it. His enjoyment was no doubt helped by the fact that marijuana and opium were so freely available. By the end of the 'sixties half the U.S. Army was stoned. Many of them were dead to the world they were killing, as high as the choppers in which they soared and plunged from the hell of firefight and ambush to the comparative safety of base camps – from insane heat and unseen enemies back to airconditioned hamburgers and Thousand Island dressing, sometimes in an hour or so. Perhaps those instant transitions from third world death to first world suburbia were the most mindblowing of the transitions of the war. Of course, it was the choppers that did it, and Page has a whole section devoted to his love affair with them, especially their Jesus nuts.

Even without additives, Page would doubtless have been insanely reckless and gone into combat situations from which wiser reporters would have stayed far, far away. As a result, his work was much coveted by giant

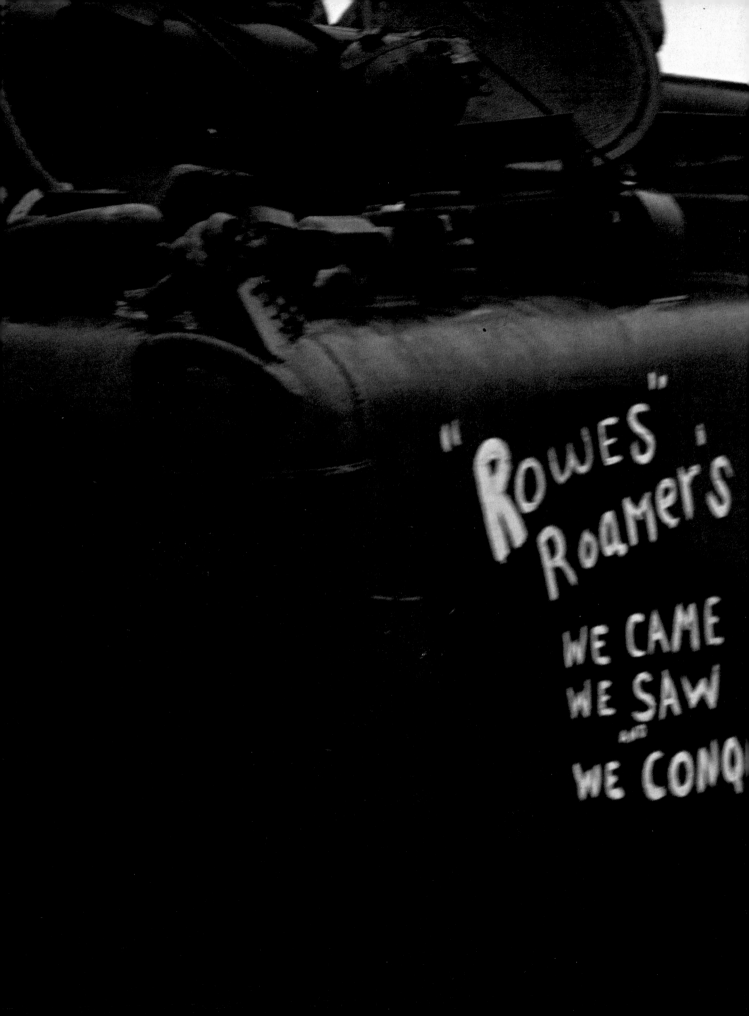

corporations, particularly Time-Life. He probably had more pictures published by them than any other freelance. They were glad to hire him – but not as a member of staff; he was just too wacky to be one of them.

It was inevitable that he would be wounded. After the first time, he simply flew straight back to Danang with his pictures and his shrapnel. In the office he was a hero: "They fed me cognac and dope and cleaned out the shrapnel and I went right back the next day. Why not? I mean, it was like an itch, and this was the only way to scratch it. It's rock and roll, you know."

Being shot by your own side was to enjoy what the Pentagon called "friendly fire." It happened to Page not once but twice. The second and worse occasion was when he went out with the Coast Guard to relax and have a swim. Nothing ever happened to the Coast Guard. But with Page aboard they were attacked by a whole swarm of U.S. aircraft. "Charming! I mean it was a real fucking acid madness horror, horror, horror. I had never seen anything like it in my life. Here's two Phantoms and a B-57 strafing us with twin Vulcans blazing, giving us a stem-to-stern strafing. They hit some gas drums, which started cooking off, and I watched a guy get his hand blown off. The skipper went up to the bridge to try and signal to the jets that we were friendlies and they blew him away. They made nine passes, and blasted the living hell out of the ship. Everybody on board was killed or wounded, I had pieces of commo wire coming out of my head like porcupine quills, a bone sticking out of my arm and countless shrapnel punctures."

His friends warned him to leave – "There's an airstrike looking for you, Page" – and leave he did for a time. But the drama of the Tet offensive lured him back. In 1969, while he was on assignment for Time-Life, the helicopter in which he was flying was diverted to pick up two wounded GIs. The sergeant who stepped out of the chopper just in front of Page had both his legs blown off by a mine. A long piece of shrapnel drove into the base of Page's brain.

He remembers staggering around trying to take more pictures and collapsing onto the floor of the helicopter. MEDEVACed to a field clearing hospital, he heard a doctor saying, "He's got twenty minutes to live." They removed a hemorrhage and tissue the size of an orange from the space where his brain had been.

He survived the twenty minutes ("How many minutes have I got left now?" he asked at one moment) and they flew him to Tokyo and then to the Walter Reed Army Hospital in Washington. Later, in Los Angeles, they refilled his head with epoxy resin and covered it with what he called astroturf. He would always be paralyzed down the left side, they said. To hell with that, he replied, and gradually forced jerky movement back into almost all his body. But the happy childhood days playing with the toys of war were gone for good.

10

Time-Life paid all his medical bills and, after persuading him to sign a form releasing the corporation from any further responsibility for him, gave him a *pourboire* of $15,000. But his wounds made it hard for him to work. The 'seventies were an unhappy time for Page, as they were for thousands of American veterans who had come home to a country which recoiled from them with their broken bodies, their damaged minds, their terrible memories and their hideous fears. Like many of them, Page hung around ("goofed" was no longer an appropriate term), with only the odd job here and there as he tried to get what was left of his head together. Not easy. For him as for so many neglected veterans, there was still too much of Vietnam whirring and sawing around beneath the astroturf. Fortunately a keen lawyer found him and suggested that – as well as maybe making some money – suing Time-Life might help to exorcise 1969 and all that. He slapped in a writ for $5 million damages on the grounds that the corporation had not met its obligations to him. He had to convince the jury that he was legally insane – could not manage his own affairs – when he signed the release. Since people have always thought him mad, this was not impossible. Eventually he won the case and, although he was awarded only $125,000, it was quite a victory for the freelance. Most veterans, sadly, had no such recourse.

It was not until the inordinate celebrations given the hostages returning from Teheran that millions of Americans realized that the Vietnam veterans had not been paid their dues.

Page was a little luckier; for him things began to look up in 1977 with the publication of Michael Herr's Vietnam book, *Dispatches*. Page is one of the main characters and, as he himself says, the success of the book began to mythologize him. Herr describes in detail the fun they all had playing stoned in Vietnam. "Vietnam was what we had instead of happy childhoods."

He quotes Page's reaction, after his brain was remade, to a request from a British publisher for a book which would "finally take the glamour out of war."

"Take the glamour out of war! I mean, how the bloody hell can you do *that*? Go and take the glamour out of a Huey, go take the glamour out of a Sheridan . . . Can *you* take the glamour out of a Cobra or getting stoned on China Beach? . . . Oh war is *good* for you, you can't take the glamour out of that. It's like trying to take the glamour out of sex, trying to take the glamour out of the Rolling Stones . . . I mean, you *know* that, it just can't be done."

Dispatches led to a revival of interest in Page's work. In 1980 the BBC made a film about him and he was given an exhibition at the Institute of Contemporary Arts in London. On both occasions "the glamour of war" was an issue. At the Institute the rather left-wing audience listened aghast as he regaled them with tales of how groovy it had been playing with choppers

12

and tanks and piloting Skyraiders. One middle-aged woman seemed almost apologetic when she asked whether it was quite such fun for those who were killed.

War has always been invested with glamour, with glory, with machismo and derring do. Page says rather more outrageously what many people, women as well as men, soldiers and civilians as well as correspondents, felt in Vietnam. It is also true that war photography has always produced pictures of great if melancholy beauty, as well as great horror.

Page's pictures show the exquisite beauty of Vietnam better than any other collection of photographs of the war that I have seen. Perhaps because so many are in colour one can feel the country's killing heat and lovely light. And one can see more clearly the extraordinary intrusion of metal helicopter beasts as they set themselves down by an ox in a green and waving field.

But there is a risk that the very beauty of the pictures can distract from the horror of what Page photographed. I think, for example, of the title-page or of the picture of the MEDEVAC helicopter coming through the pink smoke to pick up the wounded of an ambush, or of the GIs in their green fatigues sloping away through the dappled green forest.

Page would say that all he took were "reality pictures," and so he did. But there were thousands of different "realities" in that as in any war. Other photographers, like Philip Jones Griffiths, concentrated more on the civilian casualties of the combat. Perhaps Page's most striking pictures are of the GIs, poor whites and blacks plucked from the ignorant and often innocent island of America's heart and cast without understanding or preparation into an utterly alien and terrifying world. In his pictures and indeed in his commentary Page records the 'sixties-psychedelic side of the GI culture, the inanity of their predicament and the refuge they took in dope and rock. That quality of the war was perhaps unique to Vietnam; certainly it was one of its "realities."

Some of the other pictures — of the bombing of refugee shanties, of the arrested Viet Cong suspects about to die, of the boy weeping over the body of his sister — show what one might call the more mundane realities, common to all wars: the destruction of society, the death of children and parents in pain and indignity. That is the enduring reality of any war and to that there is no glamour at all. All over America veterans of the combat zone are suffering it still today and so is all of Vietnam.

In Vietnam the pity of war has been followed by a pitiable peace. Victory for the north did not bring reconciliation. In Saigon, HoChiMinhville only in name, poor kids still play, *"I gotta get outta this place, if it's the last thing I ever do."*

WILLIAM SHAWCROSS

CHOPPER BLITZKRIEG

"Coming through hot, sir" — CREW CHIEF TO PILOT ON TURBINE IGNITION PRE LIFT-OFF

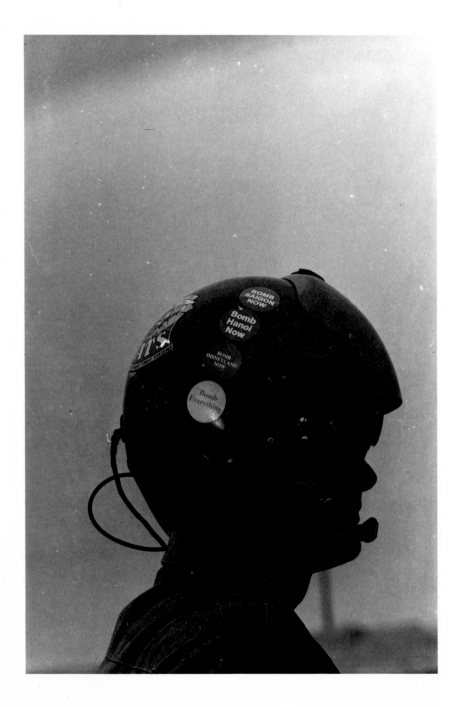

The clackety-thud of blades straining at their Jesus nuts gets everyone running hot and cold at peak pitch. Nearly 9,000 birds were lost in Vietnam . . . to ground fire, to ground action, to mechanical failure. Every grunt and desk jockey from Ca Mau to Con Thien gave more than a cursory glance skywards at the thud of an approaching chopper, be it an ARVN34, a Huey, Loach or Chinook.

Riding on the early morning mists, not knowing if the LZ is hot or cold despite endless briefings and grease pencils on acetate overlays, the constant military syntax babble between crew and pilots, the chatter of outgoing '60 fire, hot spent shells, windrush, and the knowledge that if it's a wet paddy, it's up to your thighs, chest, or above. A panorama of dragonfly-like machines stuttering into the Z, a pucker factor of F32.

Then the dreaded slamming on metal if the ship's hit, holes making windscreams in the cheap aircon.

On the ground it's always confusion, dust, smoke, unfamiliar territory wet or dry. Everyone seems to mill around in mad ant-like patterns waiting for the seething to calm down; maybe it will, maybe it won't, and when it's hot, it's very hot.

A Delta day at 105 in the shade, 90 humidity pre-monsoon, when the air can be carved up with a machete; extracting up out of 12.7 range, the airconditioned luxury of 1500 feet is truly magic, a whirl towards PX normalcy, a sense of security after the endless plod humping 20 keys of gear through the bad dream.

Always a pleasure to catch a chopper, a sinking feeling once you're aboard till you're out and then a curse for having done so, envy of those who will have cool air and water all day, a sense of commitment having fragged it, a sense of regret at being in it. Clacking here, clicking there, all four Corps were like a zigzag of tracked chopper lines, hundreds of hours scanning over a green-brown land riddled with crater smoke defoliation, swooping down to land on a mission to snatch some farmer off his bicycle, to bracket some palm-thatched hootch with tracers, or like one pilot I knew who would fly at zero feet with his door gunner lying flat on the floor taking out buffaloes with a .38 special.

The Huey was the taxicab of the war. You could spend days with one aviation unit fragging missions all over the Corps: eagle lifts, reacting to small units under fire, resupply runs and dustoffs; when there were too many WIA or KIA you got left behind on the ground. Occasionally you get to ride a hog gunship, the armoured sportscar of the inventory – but they rarely set you down. I knew a hog driver that flew on acid who would leave his visiting card on his kill; "The Psychedelic Killer has struck again!" But Command never did suss his ID.

Sitting in the door gunner's seat in a Huey fragged by PIOs of the 25th Div, getting lost over Charlie's turf up by the Fish Hook and watching those blue-green tracers of 12.7s hover towards you, no door gunners on board, just pilot and co-pilot. Groping for the 60's twin grip and feeding a belt through made me feel more useful, more stupid, just wasn't my job defending that mission. The PIO didn't know zip about door guns, just sat there gawking. Once in the same locale, five of us correspondents were put down two klicks from the nearest friendlies by mistake. For an hour we stood there waving and shouting at every passing bird till I fished the signal out of my never used Special Forces survival pack, a boyscout must; and an astonished pilot circled once, twice, and finally retrieved three majors and two captains (our ranks as correspondents).

Contour flying was the Grand Prix of the whole event. Coming in from a mission with bamboo feathers and rice stalks draped off the skids, each rotor thud a red line reading on the nerves, you knew you were riding on the seat of your pants and a micro mill mistake spelt body bags all round. But that low down it was harder for Charlie to track you. Hedge-hopping in style.

The big choppers could feel like elevators, a sky crane from ground to 2500 feet in seconds, stomach lift, eyes popping, hanging on those Jesus nuts. You would think that bigger is safer; twin-rotored Chinooks, Sea Knights, Sky Cranes stronger, can take more hits. They just come down heavier and provide more human colanders inside, like at Chu Phong when our Chinook took 60 hits going in. Charlie got eight choppers in ten minutes that morning, and we only got as far as the edge of the LZ before beating a retreat.

Somehow, when you're wounded, the ships feel snail-slow, the crew chief always seems to say only 5 minutes more to the Med; maybe it's just the hurt, the heat, thus a mirror of your own frail heart.

A bringer of life and death, the saving scythe of mini guns, the pallets of plastic water jerry-cans, half mashed, into a chain-sawed war zone D, the skyhook dustoff out of triple canopy jungle where even a smoke grenade doesn't penetrate. The late dusk extract from some precarious rock pile of a guaranteed miserable night, back to a marine-run press centre of stateside T-bones, and Vodka Collins, gung-ho back-slapping, and then, at last, an opium solace.

We still look up when one clatters overhead. I will always think that they make a great camera platform, but a better frame; the heart still flutters around them.

PORTRAITS

"Every picture tells a painted story" – ROD STEWART

It was one of those years, good and bad all balled up into one rolling stone. '68, the year of the election, of revolt, the Airplane, Doors and Sergeant Pepper, Tet and mini-Tet, Khe Sanh; an incredibly mad year.

Life got the idea from us lowly guys out in the field to do a piece on how the GIs were deciding to vote. For once the military were going to look good. The bureau split up into teams and set off for different quarters of the four Corps. Dale Wittner and I drew the 9th Division down near Tan An in the northern delta and choppered out to a company plugging the paddies on an anti-rocket patrol. We filtered down to a fire team of three draftees, two white dudes and a black guy. Voting wasn't exactly one of their top priorities. They stayed stoned day in day out. One spent the day making really snappy bamboo pipes adorned with coloured raffia, the rest of the time smoking Cambodian Red in them. He and I hit it off really well: we traded Lao Green for the Red. Evened Indo-China out for a few moments, and he made a full page in the magazine; his black buddy wound up on a Motown album cover.

26

The grunts even had a Marine of the Month ceremony for the most together lad of the moment; he got a medal and an in-country R & R before being allowed to return to normal, wherever that was.

Shortly after I got back to 'Nam in '68, before mini-Tet, I realized that I wanted to shoot portraits and do a big piece, a book, anything, called "The Eyes of Survival." I'd go out for days surfing high on a *Time/Life* accreditation card to get into the weirdest places – sometimes on assignment, likely as not, but just to get those faces, the eyes, didn't matter whose, just eyes and faces; it somehow seemed the right way to shoot the conflict.

Anticipation, fear, relief, the joy all poured out at once; you really had to focus on the people in choppers: it was like being inside a giant blender, but the light was machine-lit, subtle, with those oil painting tones that make masterpieces. The file built up; it got concentrated after field trips, scout tracks, refuelling in the monsoon, more GIs voting for no one, Ranger advisers deep in the Plaines des Joncs on assignment for *Match*, black machine-gunners stoned and leech-infested south of Saigon, and LURP deer-hunter look-alikes in the Michelin sorting out Victor Charlie for Georgie Patton Junior's 11th Armored Cav, tank drivers boring at you out of their steel hutches, the black dude from Force Recon after a week out there, legs, officers, corpsmen, ARVN, ROKs, the whole lot a kaleidoscope of survivors, dead or alive. Those eyes could have kept me there forever; it never seemed as if I had enough to make a tome.

Occasionally a few would see the light of print, but mainly they sat in box files being shuffled into slide shows, trying to erase why they'd been shot, why I'd been there.

THE MECHANICS

"Vietnam was what we had instead of happy childhoods" – MICHAEL HERR, *Dispatches*

Unlike the other side that relied on bamboo technology until the closing stages of the conflict, the average GI was a walking ad for the offshoots of NASA. They were all looped, draped or hung with the latest gismos of Western innovation, the gadgets which promote themselves from Safeway aisles and mail order catalogues. They were equipped to do a job; command had all the big toys to support them, plus the computers to convince everyone, including themselves, that they were winning, or at least envisaging lights at the end of the tunnel. I always wondered whose tunnel, since Charlie had a 200km underground complex extending to the outskirts of Saigon. The VC relied on guerilla guile backed by Eastern bloc simplistic durability. They always had the right to win; after all, Vietnam was their country, and Cong meant nationalism, something more than that red-rag-to-a-bull term, communism.

When you got down to it, it was less of a battle of the technical toys, more about the stamina of the people out there on the ground; between the folks who lived there and the white devils who had come to try and push them out of their own backyards at flashpoint. Not to say that millions of them did not get napalmed, strafed, shot and blitzed trying to stay in their yards.

Most of the time we spent slogging about in vicious circles looking for him, trying to discern who was who. The average GI had no more idea who was a VC than who was a "friendly farmer;" a lot of friendly farmers got blown away. The maxim was shoot first, ask questions later. Few Vietnamese tried living in their so-called "Free Fire Zones," where anything was target practice.

Vietnam would normally have ranked as one of the most beautiful spots on this planet. Instead, it was a daunting place to operate a coordinated anti-guerilla campaign. Vietnam was very hot and very wet during the monsoon, but during the dry season there wasn't a drop to drink even in the jungle. The hill country was ravenous: it could eat a whole brigade and its supporting aviation and artillery units alive for breakfast; the swamps and paddies could eat the reserves for lunch. Gear dropped apart in a million mysterious mildewed ways, the body seemed to grow things that existed only in horror movies. The day-to-day stuff, a shower, a hot meal, a clean rack, were a matter of supreme skill coupled with the problem of just staying alive.

34

You could not tell where the next threat would be lurking, and even the military gave up counting the booby traps. The better the toys at one's disposal, the easier survival could become. The poor Marines, with most of mind-boggling I Corps – a mean quadrant taking in the hills fronting Laos and the North – got mainly the other services' hand-me-downs. The Special Forces, the LURPs, the Seals got the cream. With a little propitious trading, a brick of Ektachrome out of the *Time/Life* fridge could become a PRC 25 radio, the top of the line Hi Fi in inter-forces communication; you could just about dial the Pentagon from paddy zero, or at least call in the wrath of God. On the black you could get a hot chopper, a can of Cs or a PBR that fell off the back of a truck on the way to the front.

America's youthful allies, the Filipinos, the Thais, the Koreans, guarded the vital lines of supply from dock to PX. It was possible to order a jeep or TV before it even got in-country: a computerized black market. Even if the bad guys had not got enough stuff up North, they could always go downtown and score whatever struck their fancy. Our guys spent a lot of time salvaging belt buckles and packs off their KIAs – traded straight in to the desk-wallahs and supply kings back at base, where the cold, cold beer, steaks and malteds took the rough out of the dry and the high out of flying, put fear back in its sticky back pocket. The machines were almost lovable, anodized black aluminium stereos, Leica solid precision-made toys. They could make anyone want to be a small boy, or at least an enterprising teenager all over again.

Amongst the in-crowd, a certain hard core of the regular heads of the press, those who made the field on a regular basis, who actually could see and dig what was happening out there, there was a mania to have the latest gismo, be it an Aussie poncho, 9th Div recondo D ring, or pilot survival K bar knife (complete with scabbard and sharpening stone and safety lanyard). Sean Flynn and Dana Stone once had a competition to see who could collect the most bars of C4 plastique. They are both still MIA.

When the Marines at the press centre wised to that, they switched to flare chutes; it took some madness going out of the way to score those spent parachutes, but they made nice ceiling drapes. Being out there in the middle of it with all that gear fed everyone's Biggles syndrome. So many of the lethal gadgets had a pure and simple sexiness, the romance of power over life, ego-saving, black and white decisive life and death, the ultimate blast, the final wave on the best-equipped board in the surf.

I am not sure if most, even in the depths of the soul-searching hawk and dove debates, really weren't out there mainly for the hell of it, for the kicks, the fun, the brush with all that was most evil, most dear, most profane; maybe in the end we were there because we had to be, because it was there.

At least you could make the most, the best of it. It was the only scene/war we had and we were enmeshed above our heads in it; the camaraderie, the sheer adventure of it all, were the biggest isms that could ever frag our hearts and minds.

ROCK AND ROLL FLASH

"From Saigon, the beat goes on" — AFVN CHANNEL 54 AIRCHECK

In-country reverberated to the sounds of AFRVN. From the Delta to the DMZ, LBJ's finest were locked into a mystic rock and roll on full auto.

"AFVN on the hour, with all the in-country and world news, read to you by Army Specialist Gary Peers . . . But first, a word from our sponsors . . . Let's talk about tracers: they sure are pretty, but they burn up your barrel. So let's use more ball ammunition . . . There must be some way outta here . . . some way to get some relief . . . More troops turned out for James Brown than for the Bob Hope yearly USO extravaganza at the Long Binh amphitheatre . . . Know what Charlie can do with this golf club, this trampoline. With Ann Margaret . . . amid the Stalingrad rubble of Saigon's 8ème mini-Tet, tracks and dozer tanks made everything a bad acid trip. . . . Hail, Hail, Rock and Roll, everyone locked on to full automatic . . . jungle fever supplied by Creedence . . . dedicated to the blue-eyed soul brother in the mess at Pleiku . . . to the jive knights in the bunker at Sanh Khe . . . and here's the Sergeant Pepper ski report . . . 20 to 40 inch Base at Big Bear . . . the Grateful Dead, the Stones giving satisfaction wherever a top sergeant could tolerate the vibes . . . Count Malaria reminding you to take your chloroquine phosphate pills . . . Junior Walker wailing point with a shotgun . . . Do it . . . Getting down to the beat . . . and the beat goes on . . . generals protesting the airing of Jose Feliciano's Star-Spangled Banner . . . Confederate flags on whip antenna . . . only the strong survive . . . The 101st

had actually owned Hendrix for a while . . . the transistor couched in a turret . . . Are you Experienced? . . . can you feed an M60 Machine Gun, a '79 Grenade launcher . . . do you want to get some . . . This is the end . . . reach out and touch the hand of somebody you love – manic depressions . . . a hard day's night . . . days are just as bad . . . at the automatic tone it will be twelve noon . . . and here is the news compiled from commercial and military sources . . . The 11th Armored Cavalry Regiment were attacked by an unknown number of enemy in a night position. The mechanized infantry used their organic weapons and machine guns to . . . Lord I'm 2000 miles from home, my feet are hurting real bad . . . that is organic . . . the enemy's offensive is of little importance . . . come on baby light my fire . . . only the strong survive . . . one sound we may never hear if we don't check our vehicle before starting . . . you never do hear booby traps . . . so let's talk about recreational facilities like bowling alleys, golf courses . . . let's talk about riding an LST full of 155mm shells up the Hue river . . . this is the dawning of the Age of Aquarius . . . so do your thing . . . the final body count after the batallion-sized attack is 198 VC dead, 13 U.S. KIA and one wounded . . . a concentrated attack is to be made to rid the country of illegal and dangerous drugs . . . the hits keep on coming . . . the beat goes on . . . can you see that I am not afraid . . . this is army specialist Donald Moore, it's 82 here in downtown Danang at 0700 hours . . . it's blowing in the wind . . . I can't get no satisfaction . . . putting out firepower in the Michelin plantation . . . 200 vehicles locked in line mowing down the rubber . . . born to be wild . . . that's what I say . . . I can't get no . . . but I am a believer . . . Uptight magazine, the portrait magazine of the U.S. army in Vietnam . . . your future, your decision, your army . . . nothing but a heartache, that's the Flirtations, or that was Wilson Pickett, sorry about that . . . even General Abrams flashed the ridged V of peace . . . for hard core Paul and his fire team at Polei Klang . . . play a song for me . . . the hits keep on coming . . . can you see that I'm not . . . just everyday people . . . the army needs recruits . . . I'm a believer . . . Yeah, Yeah, Yeah . . . and now the Go radio program brings you Booker T. and the M.G.'s; one of these nights we're gonna hang 'em high . . . everyone staying high . . . hippies converted to firepower . . . it's entertaining, music-minded, informative, swinging. The American armed forces VN network, four little words that signify six years of broadcasting to the serviceman in Vietnam . . . people everywhere just wanna be free . . . the new colony six from Chicago . . . are you returning to civilian life after Vietnam . . . can you picture what we've seen in a desperate land . . . sign up here in Danang with the University of Maryland . . . sign up to fuse 250 kilo bombs on Yankee station . . . on the U.S.S. Midway, the Constellation, the Enterprise, Light my fire . . . just by yourself . . . come on touch me baby . . . this month you will

have an opportunity to learn a great deal about our South Vietnamese allies, February 17th is the first day of the Lunar New Year, or more simply Tet . . . Tet is like Christmas, New Year, Easter and the 4th of July combined for the Vietnamese, it is a time of solemnity, gaiety and hope. It is also a time to look at the past, enjoy the present and look forward to the future. Here is a legend of Tet and a tip to make it more pleasant for you and our Vietnamese friends . . . show them courtesy and respect the fragment of peace it brings to Vietnam . . . the enemy's offensive is of little importance . . . I've gotta get out of this place . . . too much confusion, must get some relief . . . this is the end . . . and I'll never look into your eyes again . . ."

68

C.V. OF CARRIERS

"The photo lab produces enough pictures during a cruise to cover the outside of the ship twice." — U.S. NAVY STATISTIC

The U.S.S. *Coral Sea, Midway, Constellation, Oriskany, Independence, Ranger, Bonhomme Richard*, rotating the Tonkin Gulf. Yankee and Delta Stations. Round the clock, round the year; occasional bombing truces.

A thousand planes, Skyhawks, Crusaders, Phantoms, Skyraiders, Intruders, Whales, CODs, a school of destruction.

The U.S. Navy took pride in the fact that they could all let us know . . . "The weapons department maintains more than three hundred different types of ordnance aboard the ship. The ordnance ranges in size from .005 ounces to two thousand lbs." Back in those days no one really talked of Nukes. "The hundred and fifty ton elevators used to raise and lower these planes between the flight deck and the gigantic hangar bay . . . are large enough to hold a suburban lot complete with a house and landscaping.

". . . has steam driven catapults. Each catapult can take a 70,000 lb. airplane from a standing start to one hundred and twenty miles per hour in less than 5 seconds. . . . The catapults have the power to launch a Cadillac automobile through mid air for more than a mile.

"... The airconditioning system could cool the world's biggest building, the Sears Tower in Chicago which is taller than the Empire State.

"... Averages 50,000 lbs. of laundry, washed and dried per week. More than one hundred miles of piping and more than a thousand miles of wiring in her hull.... Including the aviation groups there are nearly 5,000 men aboard ... who will use 70,000 lbs. of coffee, during a six months cruise. That's 920,000 cups of brewed coffee at seven gallons of brew per two lbs. of ground."

They'd bake enough bread for Bakersfield and produce enough power to light up a city the size of Pittsburgh. "Consumption of beef would wipe out a good sized ranch."

Every division made the demographics. "Instead of using photographs, INDYS Deck department will use enough paint to cover 314 two-bedroom

homes.'' You could use 15 rolls to film an attack launch and another 15 for recovery, 50 aircraft in the air in as many minutes.

A staggering mechanical array crammed on to one enormous floating box. The ultimate Tamiya kit. The perfect bathtub toy. The only totally sterile environment in the theatre; where else could a fish-eye lens be used to full effect, where else motor-drives live clean wind-ons, where else ten TV channels or an endless chow line. The Navy made sure you felt comfortable, clean, and wanted. I spent six weeks cruising once, ship-to-ship hitchhiking from outside Haiphong on Yankee Station to Delta Phu Quoc off the Cambodian border line. You got an escort, an assistant, a VIP officer's billed-hat, and a lot of respect. The perfect harmony of men and machines. Yet is was sad to think that many of them would never really understand the effect they were having ashore.

SUFFERINGS

"Life, however, is like war: the more you experience it, the more terrifying it becomes"
— PHILIP CAPUTO, *The Horn of Africa*

Getting zapped preyed on everybody's minds. I got more scared about losing my sight. The second time I was hit by M79 shrap in '66, in the revolt in Danang, the blood from two head hits had run in my eyes, blinding me for a few hours. Panic and terror. Death was something that happened to all those people you saw in body bags. Getting wounded was just painful and a calculable amount of time laid up recovering, then back into it.

Fear was something else, something you unconsciously beat down, aware of it, let it ride you, take you, then you could use it; the camera became a filter to the madness and horror, a means of portraying it. Sometimes it could even act as a superannuated helmet-cum-flack vest. An M3 Leica saved my eye when I was on a coast guard cutter, strafed, rocketed and bombed off the DMZ. It was a passport to witness the most insane events man can put together. At any given moment, you were never a bystander, you had to be involved, be it a 21mm a foot off a tortured man's face, or 300mm dissecting a city block disintegrating. The only thing it couldn't stop was the stench of death. No smell more green and putrid. Chopper and plane crews flying bodies put tiger balm on scarves around their faces; I used a bar of Dial wrapped in a GI towel.

After making the frames which *Life* published of the ambush of the 173rd AB in the Iron Triangle, I was carrying a wounded GI with three other crazed survivors of the company. 19 KIA and 35 WIA in five seconds after the interpreter had been called in to read a sign in Vietnamese which said, "Any American read this die." Behind the message was a 105mm shell booby-trapped like a claymore.

I was shooting a Nikon one-handed and carrying a leg attached by ligaments to a GI's hip encased by his poncho. It came off. What to do? He was going to die anyway, as the first dustoffs in were filled in seconds. I'd been too shocked and stunned to really move about for a while. It was probably the most concentrated piece of mayhem on full blast that I'd seen so far. Making the frames became an automatic response, a question of composition, aperture, speed, etc., a calculated snap, confused with the primal need to help. There was too much to shoot. Too many frames to be made. No time to do it.

Prior to that, I'd got a six-page spread in *Life*, when a couple of Marines stormed a hill on the Batangan Peninsula, south of Chu Lai. The batallion was almost annihilated and I took some shrapnel in the ass, used my toothpaste sample-sized morphine syrette, got evacced and returned to the press center a conquering hero and $5,000 better off. The shrap was pulled out and I went back in the next morning to a hairier situation, to a surrounded decimated amtrack/tank unit where the CO had died with a bayonet in his hand locked in rigor mortis, face up in the paddies: they were really hurting, really suffering.

But it was the Vietnamese who really copped it. Millions were killed, maimed, raped, burned, made homeless and generally fucked over in just about every way man can contrive. They never knew what hit them. A lot of the times, as with B52 arclight strikes, you never heard the monsters. All you got was 750 lb. airmail delivery of amatol and jagged scrap metal.

Those who weren't packing a weapon spent most of their lives cowering in front of or being menaced by one. Power, the fear and loathing, all grew out of a flash suppressor, whether ours or theirs, an M16 or an AK47, grenade launcher with flechette round or RPG rocket.

The U.S. even trundled the demothballed U.S.S. *New Jersey*, the world's last battleship, out to the South China Sea to lob 16-inch behemoth shells indiscriminately onto the "friendly farmers." There were a million ways, and then some, that people and other living things could be dealt with, a soldier of fortune catalogue. One Air Force unit, whose task was to defoliate the place, also destroyed all the staple food crops, trying to deny Charlie the wherewithal to survive; they had the motto, "We Prevent Forests." The whole country started to look like a leper from the air, a series of gross malformed swimming holes, barren scrags of what were once majestic 300-feet mahogany trees. The 40-ton tracked vehicles did marvels for the eco-structure of the ancient paddy irrigation system; water buffaloes, who always got nervous at the scent of a white man, got greased at the slightest snuffle. The very air and water started to take on a total polluted glint, a deathly hue in which the Vietnamese were supposed to enjoy the benefits of a free democratic way of life. Nowhere was there purity; even sleep became a luxury, and few of us liked living underground.

The Vietnamese, whose country had become our adventure sandbox, stoically hung on to their timeless culture, bedevilled by the concentrated pap of our think tanks and production lines. GIs fired in the air to avoid hitting their "brothers," white and black fought a segregated conflict, officers were warned off with concussion grenades, men put rounds through the fleshy part of their calves to get a Stateside wound. Junk was so cheap, it was snorted out of M16 barrels, shotgunning. No one was really sane, everyone on a point of total numb shock, of hysteria, a madness that shrinks have only now begun to diagnose. Everyone lived to come home; most Vietnamese ended up with no home. Even today, they are still living in a desecrated land; but at least the war has passed out of their parlour.

On April the 19th, at 14.02 (my Rolex froze at that moment), while shooting for *Time*, my 'Nam blew to a standstill. A 25th Div C & C chopper I was riding in north of the Parrot's Beak, 35 kms from Saigon, was diverted to a dustoff for two troops who had gotten badly chewed up on a bouncing betty booby trap. Going out to help photograph the action, some dink popped off a command detonated a 105mm shell booby mine. A nightmare later I awoke feeling like a Catch 22 syndrome, a veritable tangle of plastic capillary tubing and 200 cc's of grey matter lighter. DOA or 20 seconds out from it. Dust off, dust off. The next year they installed a plastic lid and for the next twelve months my mind dwelt on the enormity of having been there. The focus was pushed and pulled until the light became pin-sharp. The sufferings had dimmed; there had been no reality, only a strained sense of nostalgia and fantasy.

98

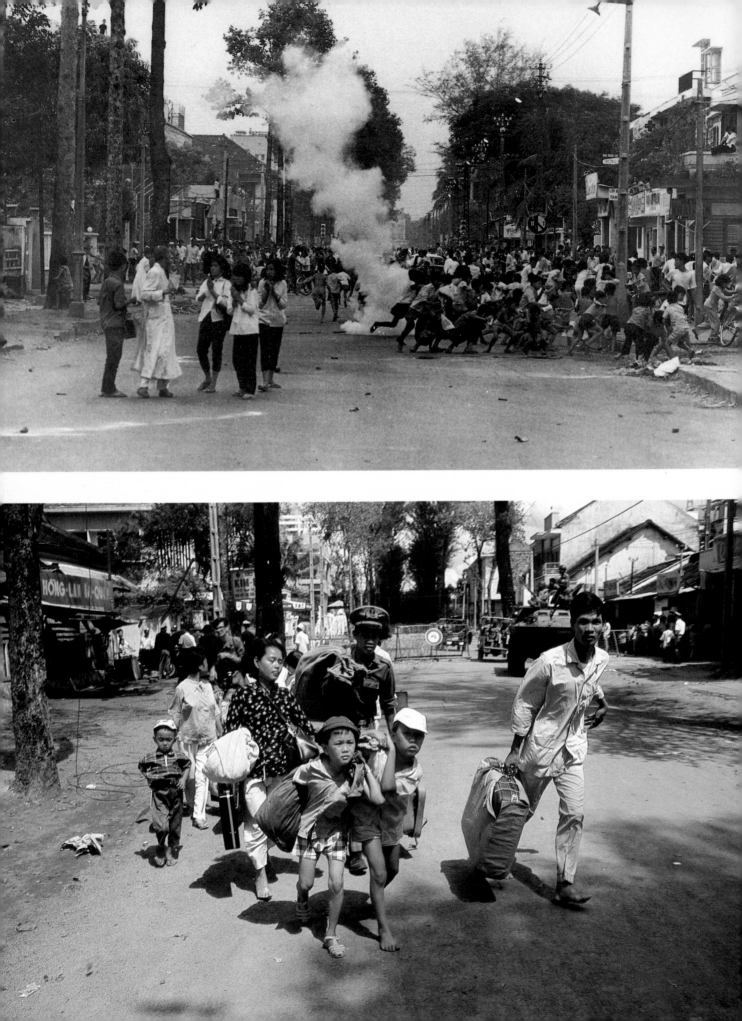

THE DAO OF PEACE

"If all religions were rivers, this is the lake into which they would flow."
— JOHN STEINBECK IV

Despite the madness, the horror, the insanity of the whole place, the war, there was an island of Peace, a reserve of sanity and tranquillity, of meditation, of Dao. There existed other enclaves of quiet, but on the island of Phoung, a large sandbar in the Mekong between My Tho and Ben Tre, peace was the sacred word. On both banks of the river, war raged; napalm dropped 200 meters from the island. Ben Tre was the town said by one U.S. staff officer, after Tet, to be a city "we destroyed to save." On the island, however, there were no weapons, no curfew and all the sides gave the island its scant immunity, to the degree that choppers would fly around rather than over it. It was inhabited by a sect known as the Dao or, as their leader the Dao Dua called them, the Neo-Catholic-Buddhist church of Dao (Tao in Vietnamese). The Americans liked to call it a goddam VC R & R Centre; certainly you could meet VC there, but especially after the Tet offensive, deserters, dropouts, families, and refugees of all political persuasions sought refuge there, for here was no fear. They lived under a straight moral and ethic code combined from all the religions of the area, to pray 24 hours a day for peace. It looked like an oriental Disneyland: a large concrete prayer platform on stilts above the mud and mangrove with tons of concrete sculpts rising from it, representing the various mythologies of Vietnam. Established in the early 'sixties by the chief monk, an ex-French-trained chemical engineer who had neither indulged in sex nor lain in a horizontal position for the past 25 years, and who consumed nothing but coconuts, maintaining a vow of silence until peace had arrived; the brown-robed macrobiotic population chanted silently accompanied by wind chimes and gongs fashioned from shell casings from the conflict, reading the enlightened texts of their sage's Buddhic Tantristic philosophies. This was the place where a lot of us would go between field trips for weekends of solace, quiet of being, alive and in touch with the self, a step back from insanity.

112

It was a break from the C-rations survival, a touch of real reality, a mirror to the soul; it was a matter of tremendous pride one day that eight of us were ordained and presented with robes and alms. From then on, including periods in military hospitals, I was simply able to say Dao when asked for my religion.

Going back in 1980, on the first free world tourist trip to the Peoples' Democratic Republic, we were taken to Phoung as part of the program. The place was still there, including other finished fantasies of the Dao Dua's fantastic mythology, the serpent jetty, the yellow peace barge with magic eight-sided peace table. However, the island was almost deserted, no friendly healthy children, or monks, and their families. The Dao Dua, foreseeing in '74 the impending Communist victory and attitude to freedom, had decamped, leaving a shrine to his philosophy. Now the few remaining devotees who had been yo-yoed in and out of re-education camps, though recognizing me, were too frightened to give more than a tentative whisper and intense eye contact. They had been reduced to a pitiful existence, making coconut artifacts from the very trees upon which they had depended, for sale to occasional E-bloc tour heavies. We then went to eat a packed lunch off the altar of a desecrated Buddhist shrine in nearby My Tho. It was the saddest day of my return to 'Nam. Peace had returned to this beautiful land at the expense of its very *raison d'être*. This was the end.

Song of the Heralds of Spring — RABINDRANATH TAGORE

We seek our playmates,
Waking them up from all corners
before it is morning.
We call them in bird-songs,
Beckon them in nodding branches.
We spread our spell for them
in the splendour of the clouds.
We laugh at solemn death
till he joins in our laughter.
We tear open time's purse
taking back his plunder from him.
You shall lose your heart to us, O Winter,
it will gleam in the trembling leaves
and break into flowers.

List of photographs